Twenty-Three

Reflections
inspired by
Psalm 23

devotionals by
STEVE SILER
with stories by guest contributors

Twenty-Three

TWENTY-THREE

The Lord is My Shepherd
I shall not want
He makes me to lie down in green pastures
He leads me beside the still waters
He restores my soul
He leads me in the paths of righteousness
For His name's sake

Yea, though I walk through the valley
of the shadow of death
I will fear no evil
For you are with me
Your rod and your staff, they comfort me

You prepare a table before me
in the presence of my enemies
You anoint my head with oil
My cup runs over
Surely goodness and mercy shall follow me
All the days of my life
And I will dwell in the house of the Lord
Forever

INTRODUCTION

A few years after I moved to Nashville in the early nineties I was invited to join a men's prayer group made up of Christian songwriters and musicians. After a while the group had settled into three core members—award-winning lyricist Tony Wood, Christian recording artist and songwriter Scott Krippayne, and myself. We met every Tuesday morning at 8:30 at a church that was centrally located for all of us.

As you might imagine, we became very close, sharing our deepest fears and greatest hopes, as well as the concerns of family members, mutual colleagues, and friends.

About five years later I was contacted by Brian Felten at Discovery House Music about writing some songs for a music project he wanted to do on the Scottish martyrs. I suggested Scott, Tony, and myself as the writing team for what ultimately became the *Celtic Cry* project, released in 2002.

Brian was so pleased with the results that he decided to ask us to team up again for a project on the life of David. As the three of us considered which Scriptures would best tell David's story naturally, the twenty-third psalm was at the top of the list.

But, while we felt that the other passages would work with new lyrics that captured the essence of the psalmist's writings, we all agreed that the words of the twenty-third psalm needed to be shared just as they were. That's how the musical setting you hear in the recordings attached to this book came to be.

The initial recording with Scott Krippayne singing, accompanied by grand piano and a full orchestra, was released in 2003 under the project title *David: Ordinary Man, Extraordinary God*. The piece was expertly produced by Kent Hooper with an exquisite arrangement by Phillip Keveren, both of whom would go on to become regulars in our prayer group!

I still remember sitting at the mix console listening with eyes closed and head bowed to the final version of the recording for the first time. When it was over, I told Kent, "If my whole career was just so I could be a part of this, then it's worth it."

To this day even after hundreds of listens, it can still give me chills.

Later, Brian Felten graciously granted us permission to make the original recording a permanent part of the Music for the Soul catalogue. Since then we have included the song on five Music for the Soul projects. For two of those projects we did some new recording.

On our *After the Storm* project, Larnelle Harris lent his incredible voice to the original orchestrated track. Then, on our grief project *Drink Deep*, the incomparable Nita Whitaker teamed up with guitar virtuoso Mark Baldwin (another member of our prayer group!) for a tender acoustic version with string quartet accompaniment. All three versions are included as free downloads toward the back of this book.

We hope these recordings of this beloved, timeless psalm will be a blessing to you and your loved ones. And we pray that the reflections and stories shared in these pages will draw you into a closer relationship with the restorer of your soul.

Steve Siler

THE LORD IS MY SHEPHERD

The Lord is my shepherd.

For most of us living in the twenty-first century, this isn't an easy metaphor to relate to. What does it mean for us to pray, "The LORD is my shepherd"?

In referring to himself as a shepherd in John 10, Jesus uses the word "voice" four times. The sheep *"hear his voice"* (v. 3), *"know his voice"* (v. 4), *"do not know the voice of strangers"* (v. 5), and *"listen to [his] voice"* (v. 16).

Voices. There are lots of them competing for our attention, especially in this media-driven age. Advertisers, politicians, pundits, celebrities, bosses, colleagues—even friends and family.

Like the Sirens of Greek mythology, many of these voices promise fulfillment—ecstasy, even—only to leave us dashed on the rocks.

So, whom do we allow to influence our decisions? Who is serving their own agenda, and who has our best interests at heart?

Jesus makes his motivation clear. *"The thief comes only to steal and kill and destroy. I came that they may have life and have it abundantly. I am the good shepherd. The good shepherd lays down his life for the sheep."*[1]

This is a voice I can follow. But wait a minute! Following? That sounds suspiciously like obedience.

It's a great irony that our greatest freedom lies in obedience—following the One who made us and understands us better than we understand ourselves. This shepherd knows what's good for us and what's harmful to us, knows which paths lead to life and which paths lead to destruction.

---

1   John 10:10–11 ESV.

As one who's always tended to be a rebel without a cause, I'm still learning this. But when I acknowledge this truth, the result is that I often experience the peace that comes from working *with*, rather than *against*, the Lord.

Doubt it? The Lord encourages us to have a day of rest. Try going without it. The Lord encourages us to honor and respect the possessions of others. Try taking what doesn't belong to you and see how that works out. This especially extends to relationships. That coveting and adultery stuff is guaranteed to kill and destroy.

Too often we see only what's right in front of us. Our immediate desires can lead us down dead-end roads—or worse. The Lord is a shepherd who not only sees the road; He sees around the bend and beyond. He knows what we need. Not just today, but every day of our lives.

Proverbs 3:5–6 says, "*Trust in the LORD with all your heart, and do not lean on your own understanding. In all your ways acknowledge him, and he will make straight your paths*" (ESV).

Put simply, this is a shepherd we can trust: a God who wants what is best for us and will never lead us down the wrong path. One who has laid down his life for all of humankind.

Where the Lord leads, we can follow with confidence. That's why we can say with assurance, "The LORD is my shepherd."

PRAYER
Lord God, thank you for being my shepherd.
Help me to trust you and follow you in all things.
In Jesus's name I pray, Amen.

A CONFESSION

Brad Weeks

"*The* LORD *is my shepherd*" . . . , which makes me one of the sheep.

Our world is currently a mess of Covid news, racial tension, and division on multiple fronts. On a personal note, my entire immediate family has been infected with the virus, and my mother is in the hospital on a ventilator fighting to recover. Families are struggling, organizations of all types are reeling, and every system that we have built is on the precipice of significant change. Broken relationships between broken people rule the headlines, and the body of Christ is struggling to remember her purpose amid all the confusion—we NEED a shepherd.

In the midst of this chaotic season, I am still struggling with the idea of submitting to the shepherd. Don't get me wrong, I LOVE that He is a good shepherd . . . and that He is MY shepherd. However, the resulting and obvious implication of my "sheep-ness" is a less attractive idea for me. There is a deep challenge for me in this confession of weakness.

To summarize, the idea that He is for me and that I "shall not want" is wonderful. But if I am being honest (even in the midst of glaring need), *I do not really want to be a sheep.*

As a sheep, I am helpless to change things.

As a sheep, I am dangerous to myself.

As a sheep, I am destined to always follow.

As a sheep, I am no different from my fellow sheep.

As my mind tangles with this reality, I am reminded by the twenty-third psalm of the shepherd's incredible and consistent posture toward my weakness. He prepares the way for me. He prepares a place for me. His wisdom sustains me.

As a shepherd, He is for me.

As a shepherd, He rescues me tirelessly.

As a shepherd, He leads me beside still waters AND through suffering.

As a shepherd, He sees me individually, . . . and He loves me.

If my shepherd possesses such great love for me, then I can submit to the truth that I am His sheep. If He will be here each morning for me, perhaps I can have the courage to accept my vulnerability. If He already knows my difficulties and has a plan for me, I can accept the challenges of today; and if He will lead me, I can follow.

So, Psalm 23 is a confession for me. While the world becomes more exhausted searching for a way through crisis after crisis, I must confess the sustaining truth: The Lord is my shepherd, . . . *and I am his sheep*, . . . and I shall not want.

Amen.

I SHALL NOT WANT

When my kids were little, my mom had a tendency to overdo it at Christmas. Every year the number of presents grew and grew, until eventually it looked like Santa's workshop had exploded in our living room. I asked my mom to please tone it down a bit, but to no avail.

Then, one Christmas morning, my then eight-year-old daughter went on a present-feeding frenzy. She would rip the wrapping off one package, look at it for two seconds, and then immediately toss it aside to start ripping the wrapping off the next one. I caught my mom's eye, and her contrite expression said, "I understand."

We are greedy, selfish creatures.

We want what we want.

And we want it now.

And we want more.

More money.

More power.

More control.

More stuff.

This is part of our sinful human nature.

If somebody else has something and we don't, then we want what that person has. Why else would humankind throughout all recorded history be constantly starting wars to conquer other people's lands and plunder their resources?

What drives us to behave in this way?

Is it fear we won't have enough?

Is it envy that somebody else's stuff is better than ours?

Or is it just "good" old-fashioned gluttony?

It seems, whatever the reason, that we all have a little bit of the farmer from Luke 12 in us—always eager to build a bigger barn.

But here's the thing. The more we have, then the more we have to take care of, store, and insure. Then the more our focus is taken away from the things of God and put on, well . . . just things.

What is this way of life costing us? Is the quest to fulfill our wants—for more, bigger, better—really God's best life for us?

We all know the answer.

"I shall not want" is a statement of faith. It is an outcome of acknowledging the Lord as our Shepherd. A shepherd tends his sheep and sees to it that they have all they need.

In Matthew 6:25 Jesus tells us not to "*worry about your life, what you will eat or drink; or about your body, what you will wear. Is not life more than food, and the body more than clothes?*"

And later in the passage, "*The pagans run after all these things, and your heavenly Father knows that you need them. But seek first his kingdom and his righteousness, and all these things will be given to you as well*" (vv. 32–33).

My friend John Mandeville has a beautiful song that says, "I want what you want more than I want anything.

I want what you want for me."

My prayer is that this would be what I want as well. For if it is, then I can trust the Lord for all of my needs. And I shall not want for anything.

PRAYER
Lord, help me to want what you want for me today.
Help me to seek you first and place my
trust in you today. In Jesus's name, Amen.

WANT

Tony Wood

I'm pretty sure the twenty-third psalm is a passage I memorized as a kid in order to win some candy or a prize in a Sunday school class. I'm grateful for the wisdom of teachers who believed in the value of hiding words of holy wisdom in the heart of a child. I'm well into my fifth decade at this point, and those verses have hung with me for the journey . . . at some points being great comfort and on occasion being a tender voice of conviction.

Virtually everyone knows the first five words of the Psalm—"The LORD is my shepherd"—but it's the next four that seared themselves into my story: "I shall not want." The unfolding of this psalm is an avalanche of the goodness of God and His great love and provision for His people. In it, I easily see His pledge of provision, peace, leading, restoration, comfort, protection, and guidance and a promise of a place in His house forever. In different seasons, different verses have been a balm to my soul based on my need of the moment. Sometimes in days of exhaustion, I would want to hear of quiet waters. In times when my life was touched by the death of a friend or family member, there was a great hope in knowing that even through that final dark valley of shadows, He is present with and actively leading His people.

Truth be told, I have at times wrestled with words six through nine in this psalm. I knew the "not wanting/lacking nothing" was because He was providing so lavishly for all my needs. However, I also knew deep inside my soul that I *did* want. I wanted a certain grade, a certain girlfriend, a certain career, a certain measure of success. Experience has shown that sometimes the wise and tender Shepherd of my steps has granted my desires. On other occasions, He has steered me toward a pasture that was not exactly the pasture I thought I wanted. Yet season after season, I've come to see His great wisdom in knowing perfectly what I needed. He has proven Himself good and faithful.

Now, when I feel the small flames of "my want" start to rise up in me, on my best days I'm pretty quick to get to "your will, not mine" and be at peace with however He leads. On my less than best days, I expend a bit more energy and wrestling getting to my final collapse into "your will, not mine." However I get there, I arrive back at a place I've been thousands of times before . . . a pastureland lacking nothing . . . a place where again I find that He is the Good Shepherd who leads me with holy wisdom and with a heart of perfect, tender love for me.

HE MAKES ME TO LIE DOWN IN GREEN PASTURES

We've boxed ourselves in. We live in boxes called houses or apartments. We drive around in boxes called cars or trucks. Most of us work indoors in another box, whether it's an office, a restaurant, or a store. Then on Sunday we go to our church box. What this means is that we spend an inordinate amount of time out of touch with the natural world.

And it's affecting us.

A report quoted in Science Daily[2] revealed that exposure to green space reduces the risk for developing diseases such as type II diabetes, cardiovascular disease, stress, and high blood pressure, just to name a few.

According to WebMD,[3] being outside improves our focus, lessens our anxiety, boosts our immune function, helps us to maintain a healthy weight, increases our creativity, *and* helps us to sleep better.

These studies powerfully suggest that being outside is good for us. But is there a spiritual component? Is spending time in nature a way to commune with our God?

Paul in Romans 1:20 makes this truth clear, saying, *"For ever since the world was created, people have seen the earth and sky. Through everything God made, they can clearly see his invisible qualities—his eternal power and divine nature. So they have no excuse for not knowing God"* (NLT).

---

2   https://www.sciencedaily.com/releases/2018/07/180706102842.htm.
3   https://www.webmd.com/balance/ss/slideshow-health-benefits-nature.

So, could it really be that God's gift of the natural world is a way for us to get to know Him better? Have you ever been to a redwood forest? The hand of humans never made a more magnificent cathedral. From the majesty of mighty mountains to the epic sweep of expansive oceans to the passionate beauty of a field of wildflowers, all of creation celebrates the hand of an imaginative, bountiful, and loving God.

Though far less dramatic, perhaps, I have found that simply a quiet morning walk through my neighborhood can draw me into God's presence. Before I know it, being outside brings me into a state of gratitude and prayer.

How gracious it is that our creative God would choose to reveal Himself through His creation. This should motivate us to care for and respect the planet, if for no other reason than to show respect for its Creator.

But, as believers, we should additionally realize that doing so is a gift to ourselves. A gift that results in better health for us and for those we love—and a gift that helps draw us into a better understanding of the character of our amazing God.

Sounds as though God really did make us to lie down in green pastures!

PRAYER

Dear Lord, thank you for the gift of our
beautiful earth. Help me today to express
my appreciation through the way I care for
your world and make time to commune
with you in it. Amen.

TRUE AND DEEP

Becky Nordquist

The Lord is my shepherd. The visual gives me a sweet, child-like vision of green pastures and a soft-faced man gently grasping his staff in one hand and petting a sweet little lamb with the other.

Nearby, a clear, tranquil brook provides refreshment. The sheep enjoy the cool water with smiles on their faces. This is what the psalmist means—right? To be chosen and claimed by the Lord, as my shepherd, means that I dwell in a rich, lush life situation—correct?

I wrestled with this. The course of my life had been anything but tranquil and refreshing.

I read the lines repeatedly: "The LORD is my shepherd; I shall not want." *My* shepherd. He chose to care for me, claim me, and wants me to accept Him as my shepherd. He wants me to accept His protection, His provision, and His teaching.

There were times I have fully accepted His care and protection—and times I have struggled with trusting Him as I neared a cliff in life's journey. Sometimes, I questioned if He'd left me in a dark valley to die alone.

I grappled with the clause "I shall not want." The truth was, I wanted an easy life without any more pain. After years of severe, chronic sexual abuse, and after being abandoned after twenty years of marriage, five pregnancy losses, and a stillbirth, . . . I was longing for ease. I yearned for simplicity. I craved peace. I wanted a break from being broken. I was tired. I wanted the white picket fence free from problems.

I dug deeper. I loved my shepherd. Yet there was this nagging sensation, as though I'd been abandoned on a hillside. I

---

prayed in pain, crying out. I asked Him to show me what this meant. Had I not truly accepted His shepherding of me? Was that why I had not experienced cool green pastures, a shining sun, and singing birds? I sat in the silence. I studied the ways of a real shepherd, and it hit me heavily as I read some explanatory words.

Once a shepherd purchases a sheep, he takes a sharp knife. Grasping the ear of the sheep, he places it on a wooden board. He then takes that sharp knife and cuts his mark into the ear. This mark is so large that it can be seen from far away. The mark says, "This one is mine."

My eyes filled with tears in realizing that my life and all of the pain was about Jesus cutting His beautiful, claiming mark so deeply into me that there would NEVER be a mistake about Who I belonged to. I'd wanted Him to do this. I asked to be all, only, forever His. He had been answering my prayer all this time. He saw my heart, entered it, and began to claim more and more of it.

The marking of a sheep isn't just painful for the sheep, but also for the shepherd. That sheep cost him. That sheep would require care and maintenance. He *loved* that sheep.

How humbly grateful I am to see that His mark is a sign of that love and protection of little ole me. Perfect God—marking His precious sheep. Painful for both. Yet true and deep.

HE LEADS ME
BESIDE THE STILL WATERS

During a routine ultrasound four months into my wife's pregnancy, our unborn son Henry was diagnosed with spina bifida. Thus began a harrowing journey of uncertain outcomes, later punctuated by multiple surgeries.

Throughout this time, even before his birth, hundreds of people were praying for us. But we felt as though we were in the boat alone in a storm with waves that threatened to capsize us. My wife and I have often reflected on that time and the inexplicable calm that covered those days, wondering how we had gotten through it. In the midst of it all, Jesus was leading us beside still waters.

Our daughter was only four when the hurricane of spina bifida blew into her life. Watching her brother endure years of surgeries while at such a young, impressionable age resulted in her experiencing what therapists call "survivor's guilt." She carried that trauma hidden from view and unresolved for many years. Later, in an effort to numb the pain, she developed a substance addiction.

For the second time in our marriage, my wife and I faced the nightmare of a child in peril. The new storm pounded us with waves even higher and more relentless than before.

Those were frightening days when we were powerless to control the outcome. But as I look back, I remember that even on the days when I felt as though I couldn't breathe, I sensed that there was a foundation holding us up. Again, even in the fear, there was an inexplicable calm that helped us to get through the next day, the next moment. In the midst of it all, Jesus was leading us beside still waters, calming not the events but the troubled seas of our hearts.

There are times it can seem as though some of the phrases we frequently hear in the church are clichés, too trite or simple to have any real meaning. Overused, they can begin to feel less true. The "peace that passes understanding" is one such phrase. It comes from Philippians 4:6–7: *"Do not be anxious about anything, but in every situation, by prayer and petition, with thanksgiving, present your requests to God. And the peace of God, which transcends all understanding, will guard your hearts and your minds in Christ Jesus."*

This is what I know: in the agony of both of those horrible situations, while the storms were raging, I experienced that peace.

I'm reminded of a lyric from "Sometimes He Calms the Storm" by my friend Tony Wood: "Sometimes He calms the storm and other times He calms His child."[4]

Are you going through a storm right now?

Let Jesus turn the troubled seas of your heart into still waters.

PRAYER
Lord, thank you that you lead me
beside still waters, not only in moments
of peace and quiet but also in moments of chaos
and turmoil. Help me to trust and follow
you always. In Jesus's name, Amen.

---

4   "Sometimes He Calms the Storm" (Benton Stokes/ Tony Wood). © 1995 BMG Songs, Inc. (Gospel Div.) ASCAP / Careers – BMG Music Pub. Inc. (Gospel Div.) BMI.

WHEN HE LEADS

Sharon Hersh

I heard it a thousand times before, but never in a place like *this*. I was in a room full of addicts, liars, and . . . losers. I suppose I was one of them, but I thought of myself as somehow better. The room was a chapel in a treatment center for alcohol and drug addiction. The familiar words the chaplain read were from the twenty-third psalm, and I was in treatment for alcoholism.

I was desperate to drink and desperate to stop. When I heard the words "*The LORD is my shepherd . . . He leads me beside the still waters,*" I felt the undertow of my life. I knew *I* had led myself to humiliation, anxiety, and dread. I belonged in this place. Shame flooded me, and I stared at a dirty spot on the floor as big, sloppy tears streamed down my face. I needed

---

those tears to bathe and baptize me into surrender—surrender to the Life that only comes from the inside out.

All the promises of the psalm—stillness, restoration, righteousness, nourishment, the "witness" of God, comfort, goodness, and mercy, never come from the outside in. In the middle of that dusty, crowded room full of losers, I heard the whisper of a Shepherd who leaves the flock of sheep who are safely in the fold for the one messy sheep who gets lost because she thinks she knows the way: "Under your skin is where I begin. Give up. Let me take the lead." I left the room, knowing I was on holy ground.

HE RESTORES MY SOUL

God's creation of the human body and all the things it can do is amazing. One of the most incredible aspects of the body is the way it can restore itself.

Every night we lie down to sleep, and our body rejuvenates itself after a long day of activity. When we exercise vigorously, not only does our body reenergize our muscles, but it builds them up stronger than before. And from the very moment we bruise or cut ourselves, our body immediately begins the healing process.

If God has designed our physical bodies to respond in this way, it follows that our spirits have been designed for restoration as well. But just as we need to do our part in making sure we get enough sleep at night to awake fully rested, we also need to apply discipline to the care of our spiritual well-being.

When I signed my first Christian staff songwriting deal in Nashville, I wanted to make the most of the opportunity God was giving me. So, I scheduled morning and afternoon appointments every weekday and wound up writing 115 songs the first year! I was spending all my time in output mode. Then one of my collaborators introduced me to the concept of filling the lake.

A reservoir can't quench anyone's thirst if it runs dry. I was writing nonstop about spiritual things without making sufficient time for prayer and Bible study. My "lake" was drying up. I decided to start scheduling days to fill the lake, to restore my soul through prayer, quiet time, Scripture, devotional readings, and long walks through the woods.

An obsessive focus on work is only one way we can marginalize God.

Time spent on social media can do it.

Time spent managing your kids' busy calendars can do it.

Addictive behaviors can certainly do it.

But regardless of whether our focus is on good things, benign things, or harmful things, the ultimate result of taking our focus off God is that our lake is going to dry up.

That's why Joshua 1:8 encourages us, *"This Book of the Law shall not depart from your mouth, but you shall meditate on it day and night"* (ESV).

We're so good in this contemporary culture at overscheduling, overconsuming, and overextending! Pray about the kinds of activities you invest in. In John 15 Jesus talks about God pruning branches so that they'll be more fruitful. Ask God to show you areas where you could adjust your day to make more room for Him. (You're doing that right now by prioritizing devotional time, so that's a good start!)

God has shown us in a variety of ways that His creation is one of restoration and life! By prioritizing our prayer and study life to walk daily with Jesus, we experience that restoration.

In John 7:37–38 Jesus says, *"Let anyone who is thirsty come to me and drink. Whoever believes in me, as Scripture has said, rivers of living water will flow from within them."*

Now, that's what I call filling the lake.

PRAYER

**Dear Lord, help me to spend time
with you each day in prayer and
Bible study so that my spirit may be
continuously restored. Amen.**

RESTORED
John Mandeville

I watch in shock as it slips from my hands. Falling from them as though it were in slow motion. I lunge forward, fumble, reach for it. But it's just beyond my grasp. The heirloom family photo with the ornate gold antique frame tumbles slowly end-over-end toward the tile floor. Impact. The frame meets the tile, and the glass cracks immediately into a spider web. While the sound of shattered glass reverberates off the walls, from behind that broken glass I see our little ones, still smiling, seemingly frozen in time.

I bend down to pick up a shard of glass from the tile, shaking my head, thinking to myself, "This is the only copy of that old family photo, so it doesn't really matter to me what it costs to restore it to its original state. All that matters is that we get this restored."

As I reach to pick up another shard, the still, small voice of the Holy Spirit whispers to me: "This is how life works when You walk with me."

"What . . . ?" I reply in my mind.

And then it becomes clear.

Life happens. Accidentally or intentionally, things that have always been one way can suddenly change in ways we could never have imagined. Just like that, what once was is no longer. And we find ourselves confused, in shock, bewildered, broken, doubting God, wondering if He even cares or sees.

I stood and looked at the photo in silence. As the kids smiled to me from beneath the spider web, I continued to meditate on what God was showing me.

Beneath the brokenness was that same photo, that same image, that same moment of joy and laughter that had been captured all those years ago by technology. But the lens through which I could encounter it now had been shattered, pieces broken that I could never hope to put back together. And these points of breaking had made it very difficult to clearly see the image, although it was obviously still there.

Yet simply by restoring the glass that had been broken and patching up a few chipped specks of gold paint on the frame, I would soon be able to experience that heirloom photo with the same level of meaning and beauty that I'd had before it had slipped from my hands.

Hard times arrive without warning. Crises makes no appointment. Brokenness breaks in unscheduled. And our perspective, our state of mind, our orientation of heart all get knocked off center.

But when we prayerfully bring these intrusions to our God in surrender, we will find that, like King David, we can say, "He restores my soul." In those moments, the impossible become possible again. Immovable mountains move. We can see things clearly—see His image in us again, because of who He is and who He always will be.

HE LEADS ME IN THE PATHS
OF RIGHTEOUSNESS

Some of the words of Scripture just don't feel as though they translate well into contemporary language. To me, "righteousness" has always been one such word. It feels lofty and unattainable. It feels like something from another time.

It feels . . . well, biblical.

Webster defines "righteous" as "acting in accord with divine or moral law: free from guilt or sin."

Whoa! Despite my best intentions most mornings, I sin before I finish my first cup of coffee. "Righteous? You can't be serious!"

Since the word "righteous" appears over five hundred times in Scripture, I think we had better take it seriously.

But wait. They say that if you aim at nothing, you'll hit it every time. So, what if we were to think of righteousness as a goal? Not so much a destination, but more like something at which we aim? What if the *attempt* is what matters? That's when the word "paths" becomes helpful.

Each of us is on a spiritual journey. When we seek God, the Lord meets us where we are to lead us on the path. Everyone's path is different. But the one thing all paths have in common is that they're long and full of twists and turns. In 2 Timothy 3:16 we're encouraged that Scripture will serve "*for instruction in righteousness*" (NKJV). God has given us a user's manual to help us as we navigate our journey toward righteousness.

In the Sermon on the Mount, Jesus exhorts us to pursue righteousness: *"Blessed are those who hunger and thirst for righteousness, for they will be filled."* [5]

Still, there will be times when we stumble and lose our way. But God is always gracious; He's there to lead us gently back to the path. For some of us, there may be times when we defiantly, deliberately leave the path. But even then, the Lord is merciful, always ready to forgive us and welcome us back on the path toward His best for us.

I think that sometimes we fall into the trap of seeing righteousness as perfection. (There's that unattainable thing again.) Since perfection is a quality reserved for God alone, I find that an extremely problematic analogy. Micah 6:8 paints a much more meaningful picture of the kind of righteousness to which we are to aspire: *"He has shown you, O man, what is good; And what does the LORD require of you but to do justly, to love mercy, and to walk humbly with your God?"* (NKJV).

This is phrased as a question. May our answer be yes as we seek to follow where the Lord leads.

PRAYER
Thank you, Lord, that you lead me in the paths
of righteousness. Help me to faithfully
follow the example you have set before me.
In your name I pray. Amen.

---

5   Matthew 5:6.

PATHS OF RIGHTEOUSNESS

Kathy Harris

When I read (or listen to) Psalm 23, I think about the Eucharist. The Holy Communion. A time when we quiet our minds and open our hearts to the Most Holy God and what He has to say to us. The Lord's Supper is also a time of sharing. Sharing the ceremonial cup and a crust of bread with other believers. And sharing our greatest fears and deepest regrets with a God who is always listening.

Of course, Psalm 23 isn't just for one day of the week or one Sunday a month. It's about daily communion with our heavenly Father through Jesus Christ. The apostle Paul instructs us in 1 Thessalonians 5:16–18 to "*rejoice always, pray continually, give thanks in all circumstances; for this is God's will for you in Christ Jesus.*"

Psalm 23 is a reminder that God has covered our every need through Jesus Christ.

The esteemed nineteenth-century theologian Charles H. Spurgeon noted in his well-known exposition *The Treasury of David*,

> The position of this psalm is worthy of notice. It follows the twenty-second, which is peculiarly the Psalm of the Cross. There are no green pastures, no still waters on the other side of the twenty-second psalm. It is only after we have read, "My God, my God, why hast

---

thou forsaken me?" that we come to "The LORD is my shepherd." We must by experience know the value of blood-shedding, and see the sword awakened against the Shepherd, before we shall be able truly to know the Sweetness of the good Shepherd's care.[6]

The only requirement for you and me is our acceptance of Christ's saving grace. Our Lord Jesus Christ not only died for our sins, but the almighty, triune God watches over us and communes with us throughout eternity. How praiseworthy is that?

In my novel *The Road to Mercy*, the protagonist reminds us that we should "praise God, even before we know how many ways He should be praised." Psalm 23 instructs us that we should also rest in the knowledge that He is leading us down *paths of righteousness* through Jesus Christ, our shepherd. And not just for our own good, but *for His name's sake.*

Did you catch that last part? We are invited to commune with our Creator for all of eternity—beginning now—while He leads us into paths of righteousness *for His name's sake.*

May He always receive the glory in our lives.

6   Spurgeon, Charles H., *The Treasures of David.* https://archive.spurgeon.org/treasury/ps023.php.

FOR HIS NAME'S SAKE

So, what's in a name? For years as a young Christian, I ended my prayers "In Jesus's name, Amen." Why? Because somewhere along the way somebody had told me that was the rule. Those were the magic words that gave a prayer the stamp of approval. But what did I believe? Did the name truly have power? Was there a deeper meaning to the name, or had ending my prayers in this way just become something I did by rote?

Then one summer evening my wife and I were sitting in the living room of our small apartment, our two-year-old daughter Stephanie perched on my wife's lap. Suddenly Stephanie's eyes rolled into the back of her head and she began to convulse involuntarily.

A nurse lived a few buildings down from us. "Get Erica!" my wife shouted. As she went to call 911 I bolted out the door and ran as fast as I could to Erica's apartment. She came right away. Once Erica was with my wife and daughter, there was nothing left for me to do but pace anxiously on the sidewalk waiting for the ambulance—and pray. After a brief trip to the hospital our daughter turned out to be okay. But all these years later, I can still remember the exact words I prayed aloud in those desperate moments: "Jesus, save my baby! Jesus, *please* save my baby!"

It was that day that I discovered what I believed about that name.

Some may wonder why we need to lift up the name of Jesus or why we're instructed in Scripture by Christ to glorify and praise God the Father. Could it be that the Creator of the universe has such a fragile ego that it needs to be constantly massaged with our praise?

Absolutely not.

I believe that when we praise the name of God and the Son whom He sent, it puts us into right relationship with the Lord.

Psalm 31:3 says, *"For you are my rock and my fortress; and for your name's sake you lead me and guide me"* (ESV).

This kind of praise causes a profound change in us that is reflected in all of our relationships and actions. Remember, He leads us in the paths of righteousness for His name's sake.

When our righteousness is credited to Him, rather than to ourselves, the Lord's reputation and influence grow. By living for his name's sake, we not only honor God but find ourselves living in a way that can draw others to our loving Lord.

There is a win-win-win happening here!

The Lord receives the praise He deserves. We receive the undeniable bounty of blessings that come from following Him. And others receive the opportunity to learn the good news of hope and new life we have found in Jesus Christ.

All of this when we live for *His name's sake.*

PRAYER
Lord God, thank you for the power of your name.
Please guide me to live for your name's sake.
In Jesus's name, Amen.

YEA, THOUGH I WALK
THROUGH THE VALLEY

The mountaintop experiences are the ones we remember.

Graduations. Weddings.

The birth of a child.

A new job or a promotion.

Winning an award.

Finally taking the dream vacation we've always wanted.

These are the experiences that hold a special place in our hearts. These are the occasions upon which we take pictures and record videos. These are the days when we feel that our prayers have been answered. We praise and thank God for goals reached, for dreams realized, and for new life and new beginnings.

But what about all the other days? The unspectacular days? The days that actually make up the majority of our lives?

They aren't mountaintop experiences. Often, they feel as though they're simply part of a routine.

Of course, the complete sentence of this Scripture takes us specifically to the valley of the shadow of death. And certainly the Lord walks with us in those most difficult days.

But I'm talking about all those other days, the days that aren't at either end of the extremes of life.

I feel as though sometimes those are the days when our faith is the most tested. We aren't celebrating or mourning. We're just grinding it out. Another morning making the kids' lunches. Another day at the office. Another Saturday mowing the lawn. Nothing exciting. No emergency. Nothing to get the adrenaline pumping.

Same old same old. Yada yada yada. We can grow weary. Sometimes we can begin to feel as though our life has settled into drudgery.

But aren't the valleys the places where we spend most of our time? Is God any less present with us in those days?

The valleys are where we learn—where we learn about patience, about commitment, about perseverance. They're where we learn how to set goals and work toward them, about how to be a part of something larger than ourselves—our family, our school, a team, a workplace, our church community. The valleys are where we learn how to grow from our failures and disappointments. They're where we learn how to be a friend, how to be steadfast, and how to love well.

And it is in the valleys, in our day-to-day life walking with the Lord, that we learn the lessons of faithfulness.

In Colossians 1:17 Paul tells us, "*He is before all things, and in him all things hold together.*"

All things.

That means that Jesus is with us on the mountaintop.

And, yes, Jesus is with us in the depths.

But Jesus is also with us when it's "just" another day.

So, let us reach for the heights. But let us remember that, wherever we are walking this day, the Lord is with us to guide and to bless.

PRAYER
Creator God, thank you for ordinary days.
Most of all, thank you, Lord, that you are
with me at all times and in all places.
In Jesus's name, Amen.

BECAUSE HE LIVES

Dr. Linda Mintle

I was a teen headed to the University of Michigan to study law. My future was promising and hopeful. But the excitement of impending college days changed in a moment. As I walked into our family kitchen one sunny summer day, my dad was sitting at the table with an Army officer. He looked distraught, and I was scared. The news was a shock. My dad quietly told me that my oldest brother was dead, killed in a plane crash over New Delhi, India, on a mission for the Army. Later, we learned it had been an act of terrorism. I froze. Panic, fear, disbelief—this had to be a nightmare. I didn't get a chance to say goodbye. We were a Christian family. This type of thing should not happen to us—or so I believed as a teen Christian. But it did happen, and working through this tragedy was difficult. Little did I know that my dad's death later in life would help me heal.

Psalm 23:4 tells us that we will walk through the valley of the shadow of death. But we are not to fear, as God will comfort us through that process. When my brother died, I was scared. I wondered what his last moments had been like. Did he fear no evil? He was a Christian, but I wondered if he was afraid in those minutes before the plane crashed.

Years later, God helped me with this when I watched my ninety-seven-year-old father die. He was clear minded and knew he was dying. There was no fear. Several times during his last few days, he had smiled, joked, and spoken of his love for the Lord. We sang praises to our God. He knew his destination and even had glimpses of his Lord through the process. At one point, he told us to put on his shoes because he was getting ready to walk again. He had been in a wheelchair for several years but knew that the release from his present body would bring freedom. He smiled and told us that Jesus was waiting. I loved my dad and was moved that he was still teaching me in his death.

It may sound odd, but my dad's death built my faith in God. Watching him approach death was strangely comforting and taught me not to fear. For the believer, death is a departure from this life to the next. When Dad was leaving us, I whispered in his ear, "To be absent from the body is to be present with the Lord."[7] My father was going to his Father. He was at peace. He looked forward to his resurrected body. After all, Jesus defeated death.

As we sang one last time, "because he lives, I can face tomorrow, because he lives, all fear is gone,"[8] these lyrics rang true. He belonged to Jesus and was going home. Yes, we grieved, but we also rejoiced, fearing no evil and being comforted by our Savior.

---

7   2 Corinthians 5:8 (paraphrase).
8   "Because He Lives" (written by Bill & Gloria Gaither) © 1971 William J. Gaither, Inc. All rights controlled by Gaither Copyright Management.

OF THE SHADOW OF DEATH

Have you ever wondered, "Why eternal life?"

In an episode of the quirky public television comedy *Doc Martin*, a seven-year-old girl with a minor ailment asks the doctor, "Am I going to die?" Her teacher, who accompanied the girl to the appointment, quickly reassures her that she's *not* going to die! But the doctor says, without expression, "Yes, you are. Everybody dies. But not today."

So, there it is. Everybody dies. In fact, from the moment we're born that's an unavoidable fact we all have to look forward to.

But it's no laughing matter. And it does cast quite a shadow. Of all the hard truths human beings are asked to carry, it might be the most difficult one. We, and all the people we love, are going to die someday.

Even before the birth of Jesus, Zechariah, the father of John the Baptist, told his son God was sending one *"by which the rising sun will come to us from heaven to shine on those living in darkness and in the shadow of death, to guide our feet into the path of peace."*[9]

I believe God knew he had to strike right at the heart of our deepest fear. So, in His mercy, He sent us Jesus to overcome death.

What Jesus did on the cross changes everything, including the twenty-third psalm. After Christ's resurrection, suddenly the shadow of death isn't as scary as it was before.

Our Savior, the One who has gone to prepare a place for us, has walked through the shadows and come out on the

---

9   Luke 1:78–79.

other side. If Jesus, the light of the world, is the One who is walking with me, I can look at death in a whole new light.

As Paul rejoices in 1 Corinthians 15:55, *"Where, O death, is your victory? Where, O death, is your sting?"*

Peace, indeed.

But that's not all! The peace of Christ is not just about heaven and what happens after our death. It is peace for the path that we journey on each and every day of our lives.

It is peace for those days when we feel discouraged and overwhelmed. As Jesus tells his disciples, *"In this world you will have trouble. But take heart! I have overcome the world."*[10]

His is peace for when we can't make sense of things, when events happen that we can't get our heads around. As Paul says, *"The peace of God, which surpasses all understanding, will guard your hearts and your minds in Christ Jesus."*[11]

Finally, it is peace for those times when we recognize the shadows caused by our own sinful thoughts and actions. It is Christ's transformational message of love and forgiveness that sets us free. In Jesus's own exultant words, *"If the Son sets you free, you will be free indeed."*[12]

So let us walk even in the shadow of death without fear—confident that the giver of peace and eternal life walks with us, both now and forever.

PRAYER

Lord Jesus, thank you for what you endured
on the cross so that I might walk in freedom
in this life and have the promise of eternal life
with you in heaven. Amen.

---

10 John 16:33.
11 Philippians 4:7 ESV.
12 John 8:36.

I KNOW YOU GOT US, LORD

Nita Whitaker

It was an honor for me to be one of the voices to sing the words of Psalm 23. These words of Scripture have especially deep and warm personal meaning to me because this was one of the mantras that came through me as I was walking through cancer treatments with my late husband. We have always known that a mother is the glue that holds a family together. As we were navigating the new roads of the changes wrought by disease treatments while trying to raise daughters, the situation presented its challenges specifically to me; it was my charge to keep everybody going forward. I didn't see the cancer as a "Why us, Lord?" but more of a "I know you got us, Lord."

The fragile human part of me felt worn and sometimes overwhelmed during the eight weeks of radiation and chemotherapy, trying to support everyone else's spiritual, emotional, and physical needs, as well as my own. Some days I felt scared, and whenever I did, without fail, the words of that psalm would wake me at night: "Yea, though I walk through the valley of the shadow of death, I will fear NO evil, for YOU are with me." I would walk through the darkened hallways of my home whisper-saying those words as a blessing over my husband, our home, and our children.

This brought a peace to my spirit and a calm to my being. I was able to get back to sleep before the morning arrived yet again, but how that Scripture that I had learned as a child in a Louisiana Vacation Bible School would come to me—would rise up through my voice in the middle of the night, as though an angel was speaking to me and through me—was amazing. Those beautiful words of that well-known Scripture got me through some of the tough nights and long days, for which I am forever grateful.

I WILL FEAR NO EVIL

What scares you?

Are you afraid you won't have enough money to pay your bills? To send your kids to college? To retire?

Are you afraid you won't pass that important test? That you'll lose your job? Or get passed over for that promotion?

Are you afraid of being rejected in a relationship? Of having a difficult conversation with a friend?

Are you afraid that you or someone you love will become ill?

Are you afraid for the future of our country? The world? The planet?

So many things from which to choose!

At thesaurus.com, *worry* and *terror* are both listed as synonyms for the word *fear*.

I think that for most of us this portion of the twenty-third psalm more often than not brings to mind the malevolent kind of evil that is brought upon us by the wicked thoughts and actions of others.

But what about the daily fears we rehearse silently to ourselves time and time again? I'd like to suggest to you that our tendency to worry and fear is evil in and of itself.

This kind of fear is evil because it robs of us good things. It stops us from having new experiences and discovering things we might enjoy. It holds us back from pursuing our passions and reaching for our dreams. It keeps us from being all that God has created us to be. As 2 Timothy 1:7 reminds us, *"God has not given us a spirit of fear"* (NKJV).

Every time we give in to our fears by worrying, we limit the power of God to do miraculous things in our lives, things He wants to do for us.

Besides that, it is just such a waste of time.

I believe this is why Jesus says "Do not worry" four times during the Sermon on the Mount, asking rhetorically in Matthew 25:27, *"Can any one of you by worrying add a single hour to your life?"*

Jesus doesn't want us to miss how important this is!

Fear can even keep us from obeying the second half of the Great Commandment that instructs us to love our neighbor as ourselves. When I operate out of fear, I rob myself of opportunities to have the abundant life God promises. Such fear is not love of self. And I cannot give my neighbor that which I myself do not possess.

I think I was in my thirties the first time I heard someone say that fear, not hate, is the opposite of love. But that is so true. Prejudice, whether racial, ethnical, or cultural, is always motivated by fear of "the other"—fear of what, or whom, we do not know.

It is through this fear that the seeds of hate are sown. Such fear is not love of neighbor.

We serve a powerful and loving God. So let us fear no evil.

But let us also not invite evil into our lives through our own fearfulness. Let us instead trust God and drive out fear with love.

PRAYER

Dear Father, thank you that you first loved me.
May I live and love fearlessly because you
are my rock and my redeemer. Amen.

IN GOD'S HANDS

Regie Hamm

The valley of the shadow of death.

That dark valley has always sounded like an ominous, scary place. I never wanted to be any place like that. But then the next clause always intrigued me: "I will fear no evil."

Why evil? Why not "danger?" or "terror?" That's what it felt like to me. But evil?

In 2003, I was lying in a hotel bed in China. The virus SARS was burning its way through the population, and I had all the symptoms. The translators had told me not to go to any hospital under any circumstances. Because if I set foot in a hospital the authorities would quarantine me (because of my symptoms) with other SARS patients. If I didn't have it already, I would get it in quarantine. SARS had a ten percent death rate (Covid 19 has a one percent). Needless to say, I was terrified.

As I lay there, coughing up my lungs and shivering with fever and chills, realizing that this government might never let me to leave, I started allowing myself to actually think the unthinkable. What if I never get out of here alive? What if I never see my home again? What were the last words I said to

---

my mother and father? Did I tell my brother I loved him before I left?

At that moment I realized I was in that dreadful place: the valley of the shadow of death. As my mind raced through all the horrible possibilities, I was suddenly overcome with a strange sense of peace.

And for the first time in my life, I realized what the author of the twenty-third psalm was talking about when he wrote, "I will fear no evil."

What I came to embrace was the knowledge that everything was going to be fine . . . even if it wasn't. And that no evil could touch me. I was in God's hands . . . even in the scariest place of my life.

Now, many years later, whenever I am seeing some dark danger on the horizon, I think back to that hotel room and the valley of the shadow. And I think about the twenty-third psalm.

And my fear subsides.

And I fear no evil.

FOR YOU ARE WITH ME

I've been the director of a Christian not-for-profit organization for twenty years now. Before that I was a contemporary Christian staff songwriter for several years. Still before that I was part of a small Christian ministry that created a theatrical production for abuse survivors.

In all three of those pursuits the goal of my heart has been the same —to let people know that nothing can separate them from the compassionate, healing love of God in Christ Jesus.

In doing this work I've learned that, above all else, people desire to be known and understood. That's the reason support groups are so helpful. Hope is a fragile thing, not to be shared with just anyone. In a support group one takes the huge step of trusting his or her hope of healing with people who've been through a similar fire—who understand the pain from the inside out.

That's big. And there is only one thing that's bigger: feeling known and understood by God. I believe that this longing—whether acknowledged or not—is the deepest yearning of every human heart.

It has been called the God-shaped hole. People have tried for ages to fill it with other things—money, power, fame, material possessions, sex, drugs, and even romantic love. But there is simply nothing else that bears the same dimensions as God's love.

So, why is it so important for this to be known and understood? What it really comes down to is this: we want to know that we are not alone.

David comforts us with these words from Psalm 139:7–10 when he writes, "*Where can I go from Your Spirit? Or where can I flee from Your presence? If I ascend into heaven, You are there; if I make my bed in hell, behold, You are there. If I take the wings of the morning, and dwell in the uttermost parts of the sea, even there Your hand shall lead me, and Your right hand shall hold me*" (NKJV).

When the disciples feared being alone, Jesus encouraged them by promising that the Holy Spirit would be with them, saying, "*I will not leave you orphans; I will come to you.*"[13]

There is no doubt that, as human beings, we are made for communion with each other. That's why family is important. That's why friends are important.

But at our very core, we are made for communion with our Creator God. That's why faith is important.

Jesus suffered on the cross and took the sin of the world upon Himself that we might be free now and for all eternity, never to be separated from God again. For us as followers of Christ, there is nowhere we can go where we will ever be alone.

"*For you are with me.*"

PRAYER
Lord Jesus, thank you that you are with me
today and every day. Help me to rest in
your presence. In your name I pray, Amen.

---

13 John 14:18 NKJV.

GOD WOULD BE WITH US

Phillip Keveren

My wife, Lisa, and I were on the verge of a major life decision. The year was 2002, and we were contemplating a move from Southern California to Nashville. Our children were at ages that made it difficult to know what was best for our family. One day, when this was weighing heavily on my mind, I received a recording for review prior to its release into the world. I had arranged the instrumental portion of the track (playing piano and conducting a string orchestra), but I was now hearing the completed lead vocal. The song, written by Scott Krippayne, Steve Siler, and Tony Wood, was a newly-created setting of the twenty-third psalm—"Twenty-Three."

I cannot adequately describe to you how the Lord used this Scripture to calm my soul at this moment in time. All I can say is that it was an extremely emotional three minutes

---

in my life. I felt very connected to the timeless story of God's shepherding of His people. "I will fear no evil for you are with me." Surely God would be with us in our adventure moving forward, if we were sincerely seeking His will.

Eighteen years have passed since that pivotal moment in our family's saga. There have been joys, sorrows, successes, and failures—and through it all God has faithfully led us. Of this I am certain: God's Word nourishes, sustains, and inspires us when we simply take the time to open the Book and allow it to minister to our soul. I am grateful to God for using Psalm 23, neatly tied up in the gift of music (a medium He knows is particularly meaningful to me) to guide and direct our path.

YOUR ROD AND YOUR STAFF,
THEY COMFORT ME

Sometimes life is just too hard. Things can happen that bring us unspeakable pain and despair. It can take everything we have simply to draw the next breath.

So often in those times, well-meaning Christians can wind up saying things that, though well intended, are more hurtful than helpful. Things like

> "God will never give you more than you can handle."
> "God must've needed another angel."
> "Everything happens for a reason."
> "God works in mysterious ways."

Offering trite clichés like these can actually trivialize someone's pain. They portray God as an uncaring puppet master and not a loving Father. This is the opposite of comfort.

Let's face it. It's hard to be around people who are in pain. It makes us uncomfortable, and we want to make it go away. I think we often throw these kinds of statements out because in the moment they make *us* feel better. If God will never give you more than you can handle, then maybe God will never give *ME* more than *I* can handle.

I cringe when I think back on some of the thoughtless, hurtful things I have said to people when I was younger. Working with Music for the Soul, I've been told hundreds of stories that are almost too painful to hear, let alone to have lived through.

That's what prompted me to write a song called "Listening," which includes the lyric "Sometimes the greatest gift of all is presence."

When we don't know what to say, nothing is an excellent choice. The shortest Scripture in the Bible shows Jesus setting this very example: "*Jesus wept.*"[14]

There are times when more words are just that. More words. That's when simply being there for someone can bring comfort that is beyond words. That's when less truly is more. Instead of words alone, sometimes prayer can include . . .

> sitting with someone in silence
> holding someone's hand while they cry
> bringing someone a meal

These are the kinds of prayers we can pray when we can't find the words.

A shepherd's rod and staff are also not words. They are the means by which the shepherd guides, directs, and protects his sheep. The reference to them in the psalm means that we can trust that God is with us even when, or perhaps especially when, we don't know which way to turn or what to say. The reassurance of God's gracious care in the midst of chaos in our lives is indeed deeply comforting.

We can be grateful for a God who is always present with us.

May we be willing to be present in a difficult season when someone's pain is beyond words and in that way reflect the love and compassion of Jesus.

PRAYER
Dear God, help me to know when all
that is required to bless another is the gift
of my presence. Thank you for the security
of your eternal presence with me.
In Jesus's name, Amen.

---

14 John 11:35.

PROTECTED

Shelly Beach

Christmas was just days away when neurological symptoms sent me to the ER. I'd been experiencing dizziness, vision changes, numbness, nausea, and migraines for more than twelve years without a diagnosis, so this visit didn't particularly distress me. A finger had been twitching annoyingly for several months, and I'd developed painful burning on the left side of my face. My primary care doctor immediately sent me to the ER with concerns about my brain.

Several hours later, I was informed by a gracious neurosurgeon that the MRI had detected what appeared to be a glioma in my brain stem. I was being scheduled for neurosurgery after Christmas. I was familiar with glioma tumors, and they're extremely aggressive.

In 1999 I had suddenly become extremely ill and spent nearly a month in a neuro-oncology unit while doctors searched for a diagnosis and treatment. I went home, and, thirteen years later, still didn't have a diagnosis. I'd researched and investigated and come to my own conclusion about my medical condition, but my doctors had always had conflicting opinions.

Now I was facing brain surgery to confirm a diagnosis for a life-threatening condition. The moment the doctor spoke the word *glioma*, an indescribable peace settled over me. I knew it was the "peace that passes understanding" the Bible speaks about because that peace was beyond my ability to produce. Grateful, I fixed my full attention on God.

Over the next days, I felt too ill to read or even to open my eyes. I lay on the couch listening to hymns and Christian music day and night. As I listened, God showed me His abundant love, grace, and mercy in my life in the period of time between 1999 and Christmas of 2013. I saw the Good Shepherd's gentle rod of guidance in my life and marriage. He guided me with soft nudges whenever I strayed from safety. When distraction separated me from His flock, His rod directed me with tender taps.

His staff protected Dan and me from harm again and again. In relationships. In decisions in our marriage. In our health. With our children. I could even see suffering that had worked out for good. God's leading—His rod and His staff—had never, ever failed, and no matter what my future held, I knew I could trust Him. Even if my biopsy showed cancer, God promised to use my illness for good.

His rod and His staff, they comfort me in every conflict, sorrow, and pain that life brings, because He is my Good Shepherd.

YOU PREPARE A TABLE
BEFORE ME

Not until I sat down to write and consider this passage of the psalm did the thought occur to me that it foreshadows the Last Supper Jesus shared with His friends in the upper room.

He prepared and shared this meal in the presence of His enemy—the one who would betray Him, selling Him out for thirty pieces of silver.

Communion has always been very special to me. The idea that Jesus would offer to share Himself freely with us through the symbolic sharing of His broken body and His poured-out blood is powerful imagery. It is only made more powerful and dramatic through His saving act on the cross.

Of course, communion as part of church liturgy is practiced only in a worship setting. It was my wife, Meredith, who first suggested to me that perhaps Jesus had an additional motivation in mind when he said, *"Do this in remembrance of me."* [15]

Jesus knew that we would sit down to a meal every day. How better to give us the opportunity to remember His sacrifice and our salvation than to attach our remembering time to the daily act of taking nourishment. "Whenever you do this"— that is, sit down to eat—"remember me."

15 Luke 22:19.

This is an incredibly simple, yet brilliant way Jesus has given us to bring the gospel into our daily lives. Through the table he has set before us to nourish our bodies, He has also given us the reminder that in blessing the food and drink we are taking the living Lord into ourselves.

After my wife shared this perspective with me, saying grace before a meal took on new significance, as it became a reminder that Christ is present at *every* table.

This changes my attitude. It gives me a moment to pause and remember that everything is a gift from God. It reminds me to be thankful not only for the Lord's provision for my daily physical sustenance, but also for the abiding love and spiritual nurture of our Savior.

Whether partaking with friends—or even with enemies— let us never forget to remember who sets the table before us . . . and then sits down at it with us.

PRAYER
Lord Jesus, thank you for having freely given
this beautiful picture as a way to remember you.
In your name I pray, Amen.

MY ENCOUNTER WITH A 2500-YEAR-OLD BOOK

Dr. Lawrence C. Keene

My mother was sixteen years old when I was born. She also gave birth to three little girls by the time she was nineteen. Every thirteen months she had another baby. At nineteen years of age, she had the overwhelming task of raising four small children all alone, as my father enlisted with thousands of other young men and women to fight in the Second World War.

It wasn't long before she had a mental and physical breakdown and the authorities stepped in and took her four little children away from her. We were all placed in an orphanage for many months. Finally, after some time, our separate clothing items were placed in four small bags, and we siblings were fostered out to two different foster homes. For three years we didn't see each other or our parents until the war was finally over.

The casualties of the Great War were not only felt in Asia or in Europe. The entire Keene family in the State of Washington also felt them. Though we didn't know it at the time, there was a name for the affliction my sisters and I experienced after these years of separation from each other and our parents: *abandonment*.

Abandonment often leaves one with feelings of separation and loneliness and an inability to form intimate relations with others.

In the course of my professional ministry, I discovered a 2500-year-old book titled the Book of Psalms. In the twenty-third chapter of that book I read, "The LORD is my shepherd, I shall not want." Those final four words really spoke to me.

In effect, they were saying to me, "I shall not want for a sense of worthiness. I shall not want for warm and intimate connections with others. I shall not want for the feeling of inclusion and companionship with significant and important people I meet." Those four words filled that huge hole within me that was formed far too early in my life because of my separation from my parents and sisters. How did someone 2500 years ago know that those four words would speak so powerfully to ME? And not only to me, but also to millions of other people—people who, through the years, have been abandoned and left broken and disheartened.

So, I have learned that the twenty-third psalm is not just a historical book. It is an existential book. It is about human existence. It is about our existence now. It is about bringing healing to a little boy's pain, a pain that was gifted to him a long time ago. It speaks to grown-ups who are still living with childhood afflictions. I am so glad that I read this old book a long time ago. I am continually gladdened when I read it again every day!

IN THE PRESENCE OF MY ENEMIES

Who are my enemies?

Come to think of it, do I actually have any enemies? Or are my "enemies" just the people in my life who give me the best opportunities for personal growth? Are they the people who challenge me to become more like Jesus?

In the Gospel of Luke, Jesus says, *"To you who are listening I say: Love your enemies, do good to those who hate you, bless those who curse you, pray for those who mistreat you. If someone slaps you on one cheek, turn to them the other also."*[16]

It sounds to me as though these people are the ones who will give me the greatest chance to model Christ and discover for myself just how close my walk with the Savior actually is.

In a wonderful prayer by St. Nikolai of Ochrid, titled "Lord, Bless My Enemies,"[17] the author writes, "One hates his enemies only when he fails to realize that they are not enemies, but cruel friends. It is truly difficult for me to say who has done me more good and who has done me more evil in the world: friends or enemies."

This brings to mind the saying we've all heard so many times about failure: we don't learn from our successes; we learn from our mistakes. That's why experience is so valuable in any profession. That's where expressions like "we learn by doing" come from. It's why I had to do ten thousand hours of songwriting before I got to the point where I was truly proficient at it.

---

16 Luke 6:27–29.
17 https://www.orthodox.net/trebnic/lord-bless-my-enemies.html.

These concepts are counterintuitive. And they are hard. But I'm reminded of a scene from *A League of Their Own*, a baseball movie starring Tom Hanks. Hanks plays the manager of a team, one of whose players wants to quit because "it just got too hard." He replies, "Of course it's hard. If it were easy everyone would do it. The hard is what makes it great."

Any of us can say we love our enemies. But loving people who are nasty to us is hard. Loving people who cheat us and say hateful things about us is hard. But as Jesus reminds us, *"If you love those who love you, what credit is that to you? Even sinners love those who love them."*[18]

So, do we want to be lip-service Christians, spouting the difficult Scriptures but ready to spew venom at the first person who makes us angry? Dusting off an inappropriate hand gesture at the next person who cuts us off in traffic?

Or do we want to do what is hard? When we are in the presence of "our enemies," Jesus's words call us to treat them in a manner befitting of those who call ourselves his disciples.

Yes it'll be hard. But the hard is what makes it great.

PRAYER
Dear Lord, when anger boils up within me
against another, please help me to treat
that person the way I would want to be treated
and in so doing show them your love.
In your name, Jesus, I pray. Amen.

---

18 Luke 6:32.

FORGIVEN

Judi Reid

For almost twenty years I'd been a long-distance caregiver for one or both of my parents. During the last two years of my father's life, he was bedridden with a debilitating disease.

I was forced to take charge when EMTs, responding to a 911 call from my mother, found my father in a state of neglect, weak and soiled. That event strengthened my resolve to step in. I hired professional, around-the-clock care so Dad could be cared for in his own home.

My mother viewed the caregivers as invaders, constantly creating conflict for everyone. She made life miserable for the staff. According to her, they could do nothing right. I was the constant intermediary.

After my father died, Mother waited two years to sell the house and move into an apartment. Any suggestions I made were seen as unwelcome interference.

The crisis point came when I visited her on her eightieth birthday. By this time, she too had become critically ill, requiring assistance 24/7. One of my gifts to her was a nurse-free weekend. We spent a lovely few days together.

Before I left on Sunday afternoon, I tried to talk with her about moving into an assisted living facility near me. She became enraged. "I'll hate you for the rest of my life, and I'm sorry you were ever born!"

"Oh, Lord," I cried, "please, don't let those be the last words I hear from my mother!"

Friends tried to comfort me, saying, "She's eighty years old. She didn't really mean it." But they didn't know my mother. I knew she meant it.

When I tried to talk to her by phone, she'd slam down

the receiver. For months I prayed that God would heal our relationship.

Then God answered my prayers in a most unusual way. In September, a nurse called to tell me that Mother had been admitted to the hospital. Her doctor insisted she couldn't go back to living in her apartment. Mother had no choice but to comply. I arranged an ambulance to transport her the hundred miles to a nursing home close to me.

Within hours, her condition became so critical that I agreed to begin hospice. What a beautiful gift God gave us. The trauma became a blessing. Time together. Time to hold her hand. Time to show love and let go. Time to give without needing to receive. Time to heal.

As her final hours approached, I became increasingly concerned regarding the condition of her soul. She'd always told me she wanted to go to hell because that's where all her friends were.

On her next to last day in the nursing home, I felt prompted to open my Bible to Psalm 23 and begin reading aloud. My heart trembled for fear I'd cause turmoil again. To my surprise, a peaceful smile covered her face. She lifted her limp wrist, pointed a finger, and whispered firmly, "More!"

I questioned her in disbelief. "You want me to read the twenty-third psalm again?" She answered, "Yes." So, I read it—again and again and again. I continued to read through tears of joy.

I was sleeping at the foot of her bed the next morning when she slipped peacefully away from earth. I'd forgiven her and myself. I was glad we had both been born.

YOU ANOINT MY HEAD WITH OIL

When I was a teenager, and even into my twenties, I had a terrible acne problem. My mom was always looking for solutions for me and at one point read somewhere that vitamin E was good for the skin.

Willing to try anything, I still remember sticking vitamin E jells with a straight pin and then squeezing the oily contents onto my face. It was messy and ineffective.

That's what this passage used to bring to mind for me. For most of us in this contemporary society, having our head physically anointed with oil is not something we have experienced.

Shepherds used to pour oil on the heads of their sheep to keep the flies out of their eyes. When I think about the idea of being anointed with oil as a way to have clarity of vision, my perspective on this passage immediately changes. Context can make all the difference.

But since we've already talked earlier in this book about my not wanting to be compared to sheep, what are some other ways we can look at the passage?

According to crosswalk.com, it was after the practice of the shepherds that the anointing with oil came to represent "a symbol of protection, empowerment, and blessing as we know it today."[19]

Again, this context changes everything. Who of us does not wish to be protected, empowered, and blessed?

---

19 https://www.crosswalk.com/faith/bible-study/what-does-it-mean-to-be
-anointed.html.

Scripture provides us with several examples of anointing. According to Knowing-Jesus.com,[20] there are no fewer than twenty-seven verses about anointing in the Bible.

Perhaps the one that we all are most familiar with is the one from Luke 4:18: *"The Spirit of the Lord is on me, because he has anointed me to proclaim good news to the poor. He has sent me to proclaim freedom for the prisoners and recovery of sight for the blind, to set the oppressed free."*

If the Lord has promised to anoint us in the twenty-third psalm, then we too have been empowered to follow in Jesus's footsteps. We too can proclaim the gospel and can work to fulfill God's purposes in this world.

Suddenly this passage is not some arcane, anachronistic verse unrelated to our lives, but a deeply meaningful symbol calling us to vibrant and active faith.

May the words of this psalm be a fragrant perfume in our lives, reminding us that God has given us His love, empowering us to be His hands and feet on this earth.

PRAYER

Creator God, thank you that your anointing
is available to me through the power of
your Holy Spirit. May it equip me to take your
love and truth to the world. Amen.

---

20 https://bible.knowing-jesus.com/topics/Anointing.

MY CUP RUNS OVER

We've all met them, people who can find the negative in anything. For them the half-full glass is always half-*empty*.

How we see that glass is a choice. My mom, Carole, grew up in a home that would put a frown on anyone's face—boards laid upon a dirt floor, mice in her mattress, and a verbally abusive father. Yet anyone who knew her would always describe her as a cheerful, upbeat person. If she said it once, she said it a thousand times, and always with a knowing smile on her face: "We all have choices."

As annoying as that sometimes was, I've learned that it's true, especially when it comes to gratitude. We get to choose every day whether we will focus on our blessings and be grateful or focus on our challenges and complain. We even get to decide whether we will reframe our challenges as "opportunities."

What I've found is that if I simply begin to think of all the reasons I have to be grateful, my cup is running over in no time with a list too long to count. Also, I immediately become aware of the gifts I take for granted. Some of them are pretty basic—like, for example, life itself.

But lest I be accused of being a Pollyanna playing the glad game, admittedly there are some days when it's easier to look on the bright side than others. All of us have experienced times when the shadows and clouds crowd in on us with a darkness that makes it hard to see anything good. How can our cup overflow then?

By remembering that the cup has not been made that could control the depth of God's love for us.

God's love is everlasting.

"I have loved you with an everlasting love."[21]

God's love is unfailing.

"May your unfailing love be with us, LORD, even as we put our hope in you."[22]

God's love is steadfast and compassionate.

"'For the mountains may depart and the hills be removed, but my steadfast love shall not depart from you, and my covenant of peace shall not be removed,' says the LORD, who has compassion on you."[23]

And God's love is selfless.

"For God so loved the world that he gave his one and only son that whoever believes in him shall not perish but have eternal life."[24]

Jesus's life was poured out for many. That means it was poured out for you and for me. How could our cup not run over?

PRAYER
**Generous Creator God, thank you for being
a never-ending source of blessing. Help me
to extend your spirit of generosity to others.
In Christ's name I pray, Amen.**

---

21 Jeremiah 31:3.
22 Psalm 33:22.
23 Isaiah 54:10 ESV.
24 John 3:16.

PERSONAL ATTENTION

Sue C. Smith

When my husband, John, prays for me, he never fails to ask God to "keep the anointing" on me. I'm a songwriter, and when I have a co-write scheduled, John prays that my co-writers and I will write an anointed song.

Psalm 23:5 says "You anoint my head with oil; my cup runs over." That anointing is a promise and a blessing available to every one of the Good Shepherd's sheep. As one of His, I'm promised that He will pour the oil of anointing and the blessing of the Holy Spirit on me. He promises more power than I can handle. Who knows what God is planning to do with all the extra? The important thing is that the next day there is a fresh supply of power to refill my cup . . . and then some!

In David's day, when a shepherd gathered his flock into the fold at night, he would count the sheep, settle them, and examine them to see if any were injured. He would anoint their wounds with oil. Sometimes he'd anoint their horns with oil to ward off insects and pests. I like to think of the Good Shepherd seeing to my hurts and needs with His personal attention. I imagine Him sending me back into the world the next day with a fresh anointing of His Spirit.

The best example I have of the way I've seen this in my life is in my songwriting. Just when I feel empty of every good

---

idea, He supplies another. When I feel exhausted and drained, I begin to write, and the desire that every songwriter knows comes roaring back to life. Whatever discouragement and frustration I feel with the "business" part of music just seems to disappear when I'm writing. I feel as though I'm operating in a realm where He is guiding, providing divine nudges, and floating down ideas, phrases, rhymes, and melodies.

Sometimes in a co-write it feels as though the song is right there wanting to be written. It's so easy. At other times the song starts and stops and restarts, sputtering along sort of like "The Little Engine That Could" until it is finished. But whether a song is easy or agonizing to write, I nearly always leave a songwriting session feeling that my cup is overflowing with joy at the opportunity to use the gift God has given me. It doesn't depend on what happens with a song once its finished, though it is wonderful when good things happen. The real overflow of joy and blessing comes in the pursuit of the song itself, especially when I feel that we wrote what God wanted us to write that day.

I believe that when any of us are living out our calling—at His mercy, in our gifting, and for His glory—we can count on Psalm 23:5. He anoints my head with oil. My cups runs over!

SURELY GOODNESS AND MERCY WILL FOLLOW ME

This passage of the psalm has always made me picture a kindly and benevolent God walking just behind me, full of forbearance and ready to forgive and clean up my next inevitable mistake.

It's a comforting thought, the idea that God is right behind us, that He has in effect "got our back."

Then one Sunday I heard the Presbyterian minister Cathy Hoop preach on this passage using a translation I hadn't heard before. The Common English Bible replaces the word "follow" with the word "pursue."

According to *Strong's Exhaustive Concordance of the Bible*,[25] the verb *radaph*, the word used in the original Hebrew, means to "chase after."

This nuance shifts and expands the meaning of this passage of Scripture for me in a powerful way.

When I was in the sixth grade at Dixie Canyon Elementary School there was a girl in our class named Linda. For some reason she had been given the nickname "Tiger" by some of the kids, and she did not like it one bit.

One day while we were out on the playground at recess, I made the mistake of saying, "Hello, Tiger." She immediately turned and started after me. I had to run as fast as I could, and every time I turned around, she was still in close pursuit. Motivated by anger, she was definitely not just "following" me. She was "chasing after" me.

---

25 Strong's #7291.

I share this example to demonstrate that being followed is not the same thing as being chased after! Chasing after implies a passion and urgency. In the case of our passage today, it implies that I'm tremendously important to God. It conveys the message that, even if it's my intention to hide from God, I simply can't do it.

Fortunately, God's motivation is love, and He will go to any lengths to not lose sight of me. No matter how far down the wrong road I go—no matter how egregious the mistake or how bad the choice—God will be hot on my tail.

There are other times in our lives when an unexpected twist or turn can leave us in a dark valley or desert not of our own choosing. Sometimes these experiences can challenge our faith and make God seem distant or even absent. We cry out, "Where are you, God?

But even then, we are never far from God.

Acts 17:28 reminds us that "*in him we live and move and have our being.*"

God is with us in all places and in all times. That's really good news.

Thankfully, I did eventually outrun Linda. But thank goodness we can never outrun God.

PRAYER
Lord, thank you that you love us with
a love that will pursue us to the ends of the
earth and beyond. Help me to love you
with my whole heart. In Jesus's name, Amen.

NEVER ALONE

Dwight Liles

"Surely goodness and mercy shall follow me all the days of my life" is not a guarantee of good fortune. It's not a biblical good luck charm. It's not a promise that there will never be trouble or adversity. Life experience should tell us this much, but apparently it doesn't sometimes. We hit a bump in the road of life and imagine that either God has abandoned us or we have somehow failed to properly exercise some sort of scriptural formula that would have kept us safe, or made us prosperous, or found us the right set of circumstances, or the right person, or the right relationship.

No, none of that is what's going on. Bad things just happen. Things go wrong, and people get hurt. That's life as it has always been, and in this age of the earth it is life as it always will be. A balanced reading of the Scriptures will show this just as readily as life experience will.

So, what does it mean when the psalmist says, "Surely goodness and mercy shall follow me all the days of my life"? Well, what if I told you that I'm not exactly sure? Yeah, I'm a pastor. Yeah, I've read the Bible through a number of times. Yeah, I've had some theological training. But I'm not a know-it-all. I'm just like you. I'm learning this life as I go, having to "play it by ear" much of the time. So, I'm no more qualified to pontificate the full meaning of life as the next guy. I'm still figuring it out, too.

Before frustration takes over and you stop reading, let me tell you that, based on my life experience so far, as well as my theological training and what little knowledge I have of the Scriptures, I'm going to venture an educated guess. Is that fair enough? Let me suggest, based on all of the above, that there is this great love that must surely underlie all of life, all of creation, all of the universe. And I think this great love not only sets all of this in motion but also, in some mysterious way, is walking with us as we make our way through the ups and downs of this thing we call life.

Of course, we call this great love "God." And, just as we believe from the Scriptures that God is love, we also believe that God is goodness and God is mercy. So, the psalmist is expressing his belief that God is walking with us through this life. Comforting us, embracing us, picking us up, empowering us, leading us, guiding us, being there. It's not a guarantee of good fortune. It's not a good luck charm. But it is a promise that we are not alone on this journey. Never alone. Never, ever alone.

ALL THE DAYS OF MY LIFE

There are days when I wake up feeling excited. Maybe it's the first day of a special vacation I've been looking forward to. Maybe I've got tickets to go see one of my favorite recording artists in concert. Or maybe it's just a beautiful, sunny day and I can't wait to get outside!

Then there are days when my first conscious thought is uneasiness. It might be that uncomfortable situation at work that I need to confront. Perhaps a loved one is facing surgery. Or there's that unexpected major expense that has me worried about how I'm going to pay this month's bills.

But whether this is a day you've been looking forward to or a day you've been dreading, one thing is still true: this is a day that the Lord has made and given to us.

If you grew up in the church—or even if you didn't—you are probably familiar with the children's song "This Is the Day": "This is the day that the Lord has made. We will rejoice and be glad in it."

This simple children's song reminds us that God is with us every day. In fact, God literally "makes time" for us every day. First of all by having created the world, including us! Then, second, by promising to be with us in every moment of every day. These are things for which we can always be grateful.

If there is one thing I've learned, it's that gratitude can make any day better. Taking time to think about what I'm grateful for immediately changes my outlook, no matter what kind of day I'm facing.

My friend Lisa and I were talking one time about gratitude.

She shared with me that she begins every day when she first awakens by saying out loud, "And a bonus!" She said that this phrase immediately shifts her perspective and reminds her to not take the day for granted.

As opposed to beginning the day with a sense of entitlement, this struck me as a great way to begin each day by acknowledging that the Lord has given us a new gift. So, I started doing it every day, and it has made a difference for me, too!

Of course, it shouldn't stop there. I need to make spending time with the Lord a daily commitment. It's so easy to jump into my day, and before I know it, I'm busy with this, that, and the other thing.

First Chronicles 16:11 says, "*Seek the LORD and his strength; seek his presence continually!*" (ESV).

It takes discipline to make room for God in our lives. But if he is Lord of *all* the days of our lives—not just Sunday—then the least I can do is offer my daily devotion in return.

PRAYER

Lord, thank you that you promise to be
with me all the days of my life. Help me to make
spending time with you a priority so that our
relationship is a two-way street every day.
In Jesus's name, Amen.

DADDY AND PSALM 23

Marnie Ferree

I know it sounds heretical, but the truth is that Psalm 23 has never been one of my favorites. I like the familiarity of the verses, but they aren't especially significant to me personally. So I had no idea what I would share, until I remembered how much the passage meant to my daddy during his last days.

Suddenly, I had a clear image of sitting beside my father's hospital bed on a small upholstered footstool with gold fringe, the one that's in my living room now. It had been lowered as close to the floor as it would go to lessen his chance of falling when he was restless and tried to get out of bed. He was in the last stage of Alzheimer's, which for him had been a blessedly rapid decline after several years of remaining very functional post-diagnosis.

My dad was especially agitated that day, he couldn't speak coherently, and it wasn't clear how much he could understand, but I knew how deeply he loved Scripture. I picked up his worn leather Bible and began to read, starting with many other psalms first—ones that I knew he loved and had preached about dozens of times. He quieted at the sound of my voice and perhaps the familiar cadence of the words, but otherwise he didn't respond.

Then I turned to the twenty-third psalm. As I begin to read, I was startled to hear him join me. His eyes remained closed, but he recited the psalm perfectly in his beautiful baritone voice, weaker now, but crystal clear. When we got to the end of the psalm and I began to flip to another selection, he put out his hand to stop me. I asked if he wanted me to read Psalm 23 again, and his hand fluttered against the thin page.

Over the next week I read my daddy the twenty-third psalm dozens of times every day. With each reading he would recite the words, too, until day by day he got weaker and then slipped beyond hearing anything.

When my daddy died on March 1, 2011, my brothers and I included the twenty-third psalm in his memorial service. We sat together in a row with our spouses, and as a dear family friend started the familiar words, I, then the brother sitting next to me, and then our other brother farther down the row spontaneously begin to say them out loud.

"The LORD is my shepherd."

AND I WILL DWELL
IN THE HOUSE OF THE LORD

You've probably seen it. You may even have one like it in your home. It's a sign that has the Scripture from Joshua 24:15.

It says, *"As for me and my house, we will serve the LORD"* (NKJV).

It's what I call planting a flag. It says to everyone who enters your home, "This is what I believe. This is what I stand for."

Of course, it also serves on those days when we ourselves need a reminder of what it is we believe and what it is we stand for.

But there's a danger in that, too. It's the danger of routine.

Things you see every day have a tendency to magically disappear. They sort of fade into the overall visual background. I know there are about a dozen pictures and cards on the front and sides of our refrigerator. I "see" them every day. But for the life of me, I couldn't tell you what most of them are. Except maybe for the cow card I got for Father's Day.

(To prove my point, I just went upstairs to check—I was wrong. There are *thirty-four* pictures and cards on the refrigerator!)

This is the ocular equivalent of taking things for granted.

And if we're not careful, this can happen in other areas of our life, too. If you're married, are you serving the Lord with the way you treat your spouse? If you're a parent, are you serving the Lord with the way you treat your children? Or maybe you live with a parent. Are you serving the Lord in that relationship? How about your neighbors? Are you serving the Lord with the way you invest your free time?

If we want to dwell in the house of the Lord, then maybe we need to get a head start on that by making sure our house is a place where the Lord would feel at home.

What's true for our home is also true for our workplace and our church, both places where routine can cause us to occasionally slacken up.

It's important to ask myself from time to time whether the Lord would feel at home in my church and whether I'm doing my part to make it a place where Jesus would feel welcome.

Fortunately, loving us is not routine for God. It's His very nature. He can't help it. He sent His Son to show us just how much He loves us.

That Son, Jesus, says in John 14:2–4, "*In my Father's house are many rooms. If it were not so, would I have told you that I go to prepare a place for you? And if I go and prepare a place for you, I will come again and will take you to myself, that where I am you may be also*" (ESV).

There it is—the promise that we will one day dwell in the house of the Lord.

Our picture is on the Lord's refrigerator. And He *never* takes us for granted.

PRAYER
Lord, thank you for the promise
of heaven and an eternity spent with you.
In Jesus's name, Amen.

FINALLY HOME
Carmen Leal Scott

My father was born and raised in New Orleans, where handsome Creole men with brown skin, twinkling eyes, and white teeth were envied and admired. He was at home in his city and the flamboyant culture until he joined the army during World War II. Daddy spent his four years as an enlisted man doing tasks beneath his intelligence and college education because of the color of his skin.

He eventually married my mom, and after a brief time in New Orleans they moved back to her family home in Kansas in 1952. We lived in a neighborhood where most of the people were of varying shades of brown. Every "colored person" who wanted to earn decent money took a government job. Daddy worked at the post office, an ill-chosen career he suffered through for over forty years. Having eight children was an incentive to keep the best paying job you could find.

A hard worker, but one who never felt at home in that job or in his neighborhood, Daddy was complex, opinionated, and argumentative. Over the years he went from being called unmentionable words to "colored" to "black" and finally to "African American," a term he particularly hated because he'd never been to Africa. When he was finally diagnosed as bipolar at seventy, this answered a multitude of questions, and I had a greater understanding of why our proud but tortured father never felt at home in this world. He died suddenly of an aneurysm at the age of eighty, but that last decade had been his best ten years, thanks to great doctors and medication.

A devout Catholic, every year he'd taken one precious week of his vacation time to walk the Stations of the Cross during Holy Week. For his funeral service, my older sister assigned each member of the family a role. I sang "The Lord's Prayer" and read Psalm 23. I managed to stay dry-eyed through the song and the reading, . . . until I got to the closing words: "I will dwell in the house of the LORD forever."

I stood at the podium on the altar in the sanctuary where Daddy had spent so much time in silent prayer or as an usher each week or arguing with a priest about some forgotten triviality. That morning a piece of the puzzle of his earthly existence fell into place. With tears streaming down my face that mirrored his café au lait hue, I knew that the only place this conflicted man had ever felt at home was in God's presence. As grieved as I was, knowing he'd never bowl in another tournament, play the saxophone badly, or see my sons graduate, I felt at peace. I knew that without a doubt Daddy was someplace without racism or mental illness. He was not only in the house of the Lord—where he would be forever—but he was waiting for us to join him. He was finally home.

FOREVER

"Forever and ever amen!"

Grace was a ninety-five-year-old woman who sat in the same chair every Wednesday morning at the nursing home where I visited to play piano for a worship service. Even though it's been almost thirty years since I've seen her. it still seems like yesterday whenever I think of her.

Every week as part of the service we would recite the Lord's prayer, and at the conclusion of the prayer Grace would sound off in her loud clear voice with the unmistakable New England accent, "Forevah and evah amen!"

Forever is a long time. Too long to wrap our minds around. Let's face it. For us human beings, time is a weird deal.

If we're doing something that we don't enjoy, a half hour can feel like three days. If we're doing something we love and want the time to stretch out, a half hour can feel like three minutes.

Perhaps you've heard it said that time heals all wounds.

According to my friend Dr. Doris Sanford, that isn't the case. "Time heals nothing," she states flatly. "Time is neutral. You've got to deal with your stuff or you won't heal."

Not very comforting. But, happily, the reference to time that ends the twenty-third psalm *is* comforting!

"Forever" in this context means that there is no point in the future when the Lord will not be with us. Though we don't know what is to come, we have the certainty of Christ's presence with us in all of it.

In the Gospel of Matthew, Jesus says. *"Surely I am with you always, to the very end of the age."*[26]

John Oxenham's 1908 hymn proclaims that "In Christ There is No East or West." Forever is the "no east or west" of time.

While we get to live only in the moment, our Creator lives simultaneously in the past, present, and future.

Just as we take solace from how God has comforted us in the past and how we are encouraged by a sense of God's being with us in the present, we can also take comfort in knowing that God is out in front of us. To our Lord there is no such thing as the future. He's already there.

With this promise in hand, we need have no fear of tomorrow.

While in his eighties, my friend Bill Allen once told me, "At the end of the day I get down on my knees and thank God for the day that I've just lived. Then I give the night to him and say I'm going to bed. I'm going to rest. You take it from here."

That's what "forever" means at the end of the psalm. Have no fear of the future. I'll take it from here. You can rest and have peace.

Now *that's* comforting.

PRAYER

Dear Lord, thank you that you know every
hair on my head and every moment of time
that is to come. Please help me to trust you
for tomorrow and live in gratitude today.
In Jesus's precious name I pray, Amen.

---

26 Matthew 28:20.

AMEN

"Amen." It literally means "so be it."

This is our affirmation that all is God's. God is sovereign, and all things are His.

God doesn't *need* our stamp of approval. But our "Amen" is us giving it anyway.

"Amen" is us relinquishing any illusion of control and saying, "Just as you would have it, Lord."

"Amen" is our trusting in the God who created the universe to know better than we do.

"Amen" is our trusting in a God who loves us more than we could possibly imagine.

"Amen" is our proclamation that there is no word more final than that of the Lord.

Our "Amen" is an act of gratitude, our responding as we are encouraged to do by the apostle Paul in 1 Thessalonians 5:18 to *"give thanks in all circumstances; for this is God's will for you in Christ Jesus."*

Our "Amen" is an acknowledgment of the profound truth of Romans 8:28 that *"in all things God works for the good of those who love him, who have been called according to his purpose."*

"Amen" says, "As you wish, Lord."

"Amen" admits our limitations and recognizes the scope of God's unlimited vision.

"Amen" is our vote of confidence in the One who hung the moon and the stars.

With "Amen," we obediently proclaim that there is no sassing God!

It is God who gets the last word.

And so, Hallelujah!

Praise the Lord!

Thanks be to God!

So be it!

Amen.

PRAYER

Dear God. Thank you that you have given me
your word and the assurance that I can
trust You in all things. May I walk in that
conviction today and every day. In the precious
and Holy name of Jesus I pray, Amen.

SONG CREDITS

Twenty-Three
Scott Krippayne version

Lyric: The Twenty-Third Psalm, NJKV
Songwriters: Scott Krippayne, Steve Siler, and Tony Wood
Executive Producers: Brian Felten and Steve Siler
Produced by Kent Hooper
Recorded at The House of Big, Franklin, TN, Oceanway Studios,
Nashville, TN, and Wildwood Recording, Franklin, TN
Orchestra arranged and conducted by Phillip Keveren
Vocalist: Scott Krippayne
Piano: Phillip Keveren

Orchestra: David Davidson, David Angell,
Bruce Christensen, Bruce Sweetman, David Hancock,
Idalyn Besser, Elisabeth Stewart, Carolyn Hancock,
Kristyn Wilkinson, Beverly Drukker, Monisa Angell,
Anthony Lamarchina, Alison Gooding, John Catchings,
Karen Winklemann, Zeneca Bowers, Christian Teal,
Erin Hall, Clara Olson, Anne E. Page,
Roger Spencer, Ann Richards, Ellen Menking,
Elizabeth Lamb, and Bill Woodworth

Twenty-Three
Nita Whitaker version

Lyric: The Twenty-Third Psalm, NJKV

Songwriters: Scott Krippayne, Steve Siler, and Tony Wood

Produced by Kent Hooper and Steve Siler

Quartet arranged by Phillip Keveren

Guitar and String Quartet Recorded at The House of Big, Franklin, TN

Vocal recorded by Gary Griffin at The Hall of Supreme Harmony, Los Angeles, CA

Vocalist: Nita Whitaker

Guitar: Mark Baldwin

The Quartet: David Davidson, David Angell, Monisa Angell, and Sari Reist

Twenty-Three
Larnelle Harris version

Lyric: The Twenty-Third Psalm, NJKV

Songwriters: Scott Krippayne, Steve Siler, and Tony Wood

Executive Producers: Brian Felten and Steve Siler

Produced by Kent Hooper

Recorded at The House of Big, Franklin, TN, Oceanway Studios, Nashville, TN, and Wildwood Recording, Franklin, TN

Orchestra arranged and conducted by Phillip Keveren

Vocalist: Larnelle Harris

Piano: Phillip Keveren

Orchestra: David Davidson, David Angell,
Bruce Christensen, Bruce Sweetman, David Hancock,
Idalyn Besser, Elisabeth Stewart, Carolyn Hancock,
Kristyn Wilkinson, Beverly Drukker, Monisa Angell,
Anthony Lamarchina, Alison Gooding, John Catchings,
Karen Winklemann, Zeneca Bowers, Christian Teal,
Erin Hall, Clara Olson, Anne E. Page,
Roger Spencer, Ann Richards, Ellen Menking,
Elizabeth Lamb, and Bill Woodworth

Twenty-Three
A reading of the Twenty-Third Psalm

Spoken by Darrell Harris
Recorded at The House of Big, Franklin, TN

CONTRIBUTING GUEST AUTHORS

Shelly Beach

is an award-winning author of eight books,
as well as a speaker, consultant, and educator.
shellybeachonline.com

Marnie C. Ferree

is the author of *No Stones—Women Redeemed
from Sexual Addiction* and the Founder and
Director of Bethesda Workshops.
bethesdaworkshops.org

Regie Hamm

is a multi-award-winning songwriter,
recording artist, author, and blogger.
regiehammblog.wordpress.com/about/

Kathy Harris

lives in Nashville, TN, and works as a marketing
director in the entertainment business.
She is also the author of two Christian novels,
The Road to Mercy and *Deadly Commitment*,
the first book in her suspense series.
kathyharrisbooks.com

Sharon Hersh

is a licensed professional counselor, an adjunct professor in graduate counseling programs, a sought-after speaker, and the author of several books, including *Belonging: Finding the Way Back to One Another, The Last Addiction: Why Self Help Is Not Enough, Bravehearts: Unlocking the Courage to Love with Abandon*, and the award-winning *Mothering Without Guilt.* Sharon lives in Lone Tree, CO. sharonhersh.com

Rev. Dr. Lawrence C. Keene

is an author, a retired sociology professor, and a Disciples of Christ minister. lckeen@aol.com

Phillip Keveren

is an arranger, composer, orchestrator, and music producer. phillipkeveren.com

Dwight Liles

is a pastor in the Cumberland Presbyterian Church and the writer of hundreds of recorded Christian songs, including the beloved hymn "We are an Offering." dwightliles.com

John Mandeville
is a pastor, worship leader,
songwriter, and recording artist.
facebook.com/john.mandeville.music

Linda Mintle, Ph.D.
is an author, speaker, university professor,
radio show host, and licensed therapist.
drlindamintle.com

Becky Nordquist
is a singer, songwriter, author,
and worship leader.
beckynordquist.com

Judi Reid
is an author, life coach,
and founder of Women of Value.
womenofvalue.org/about

Carmen Leal Scott
is a speaker and the published author of nine
books and dozens of articles and devotionals.
She lives in Wisconsin and has become
a reluctant gardener and dog rescuer.
carmenlealwrites@gmail.com

Sue C. Smith

is a multi-award-winning Christian songwriter, author, and Founder and Director of Write about Jesus, an annual Christian songwriter conference in St. Charles, MO.
suecsmithsongwriter.com and writeaboutjesus.com

Brad Weeks

is a businessman, an investor in people, a father, and a husband. He is full of hope and is learning to forgive and to be forgiven each day.

Nita Whitaker

is an accomplished vocalist, actress, and author. She is the mother of two beautiful emerging stars, Skye and Liisi LaFontaine.
nitawhitaker.com

Tony Wood

is a multi-award-winning songwriter with over thirty #1 songs to his credit.
tonywoodonline.com

ACKNOWLEDGMENTS

The author would like to thank:

All the guest contributors for generously sharing your wisdom and friendship, Joseph Northcut for all the encouragement and for being the first reader, and Tim Beals and the talented team at Credo House Publishers.

Our incredible music production team, including producer Kent Hooper and arranger Phillip Keveren and all the amazing musicians and technicians who share their skill with Music for the Soul.

Scott Krippayne, Nita Whitaker, and Larnelle Harris for their incomparable vocal performances.

Brian Felten, who initially asked me, along with Scott and Tony Wood, the best co-writers anyone could ask for, to write songs based on the life of King David. Thanks to David for some pretty amazing source material.

The Music for the Soul leadership team: Sue Foster, Shelly Beach, Susan Brantley, John Cozart, Judi Reid, and Kathleen Curzon, The Wednesday Morning Prayer group, and all those who support Music for the Soul with your prayers and your donations. We couldn't do it without you.

Thanks to my Meredith for being in this journey with me. I love you.

Finally, thanks and praise to Jesus Christ for setting me free.

ALSO FROM
MUSIC FOR THE SOUL

Songs and readings.

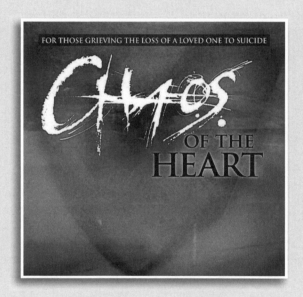

"You have captured the survivor experience with an understanding only God could have given to you."

LINDA FLATT,
AMERICAN FOUNDATION FOR SUICIDE PREVENTION-NEVADA

musicforthesoul.org/resources/chaos-of-the-heart